COMMON CORE LANGUAGE

Homonyms, Homographs, and Homophones

ELEMENTARY WORKBOOK

101 Skill-Building Practice Exercises

for Grade 3, Grade 4, and Grade 5

ISBN 978-1493587308

CONTENTS

INTRODUCTION
For Parents, Teachers, and Tutors

What are Homophones, Homographs, and Homonyms?

Homophones are words that sound the same, but have different meanings. The words *write* and *right* are homophones. Homographs are words that are spelled the same, but have different meanings. For example, the word *close* can mean "near" or "to shut." Notice that the pronunciation of *close* is different depending on its meaning. If homographs are spelled the same and sound the same, they are also homonyms. For example, the word *sweet* can mean "tasting of sugar" or "kind."

Building Skills

The exercises in this book are divided into 10 levels that progress from easy to advanced. Within each level, there are 10 different exercises covering homonyms, homophones, and homographs. The table below summarizes the general differences between each level.

Level	Difficulty	Features
Levels 1 to 3	Easy	- Grade 2 or 3 vocabulary and reading level - Simpler questions and tasks - Lower demand on students - More guided tasks
Levels 4 to 7	Moderate	- Grade 3 or 4 vocabulary and reading level - Simple to moderate questions and tasks - Higher demand on students - More student writing required
Levels 8 to 10	Advanced	- Grade 5 or higher vocabulary and reading level - Moderate to complex questions and tasks - Higher demand on students - More independent thinking required - More student writing required

At the easy levels, students will gain the foundation needed to identify, understand, and use homophones, homographs, and homonyms. Students will apply and build on these language skills as they move through the levels, while also building their vocabulary. With this leveled approach and focus, students will expand their vocabulary and language skills and advance to a level of ability that reaches and then exceeds their grade level.

Level 1

Exercises 1 to 10

Difficulty: ★☆☆

Building Your Vocabulary

As you complete the exercises, list any words you have trouble with below. Draw a picture or write down the meaning of each word.

Exercise 1

Circle the correct way to spell the name of the word shown by each picture.

	bee be
	pair pear
	bare bear
	rose rows
	bread bred

Exercise 2

Circle the two words in each list that sound the same. Then write a sentence using one of the words you circled.

 Read each list of words out loud. Focus on the sound of each word.

1 hard   (here)   hair   (hear)

I could not hear the music.

2 toe   two   too   tea

_____

3 wire   wear   where   wore

_____

4 win   one   own   won

_____

5 tee   tie   toe   tea

_____

6 now   new   knew   know

_____

Exercise 3

Use the two given words to complete each sentence. Write the missing words on the lines.

1 eye   I

It hurt when _____ got sand in my _____.

2 not   knot

I could _____ untie the _____.

3 sea   see

Josie had always wanted to _____ the _____.

4 no   know

I did not _____ there was _____ milk left.

5 red   read

I _____ a book about a little_____ car.

6 for   four

I saved _____ seats _____ my friends.

Exercise 4

Circle the word in each sentence that is used incorrectly. Then rewrite the sentence using the correct word.

 One of the words in each sentence is spelled like another word that sounds the same. Find the word that has the wrong spelling.

1 I read a funny (tail) about a bear.

I read a funny tale about a bear.

2 The flag is red, white, and blew.

_____

3 Jim got a letter in the male.

_____

4 That is my bag over their.

_____

5 I said high to the bus driver.

_____

6 I was tired, sew I went to bed.

_____

Exercise 5

Choose the best answer to each question.

1   Which sentence uses the underlined word correctly?

     Ⓐ   I went to the store to <u>by</u> milk.

     Ⓑ   I went to the store to <u>boy</u> milk.

     Ⓒ   I went to the store to <u>buy</u> milk.

     Ⓓ   I went to the store to <u>bye</u> milk.

2   Which sentence uses the underlined word correctly?

     Ⓐ   I went <u>to</u> the beach last week.

     Ⓑ   I went <u>two</u> the beach last week.

     Ⓒ   I went <u>too</u> the beach last week.

     Ⓓ   I went <u>tow</u> the beach last week.

3   Which sentence uses the underlined words correctly?

     Ⓐ   The <u>sum</u> of the two numbers was <u>ate</u>.

     Ⓑ   The <u>sum</u> of the two numbers was <u>eight</u>.

     Ⓒ   The <u>some</u> of the two numbers was <u>ate</u>.

     Ⓓ   The <u>some</u> of the two numbers was <u>eight</u>.

4   Which sentence uses the underlined words correctly?

     Ⓐ   Mrs. Davidson has one daughter and <u>for</u> <u>sons</u>.

     Ⓑ   Mrs. Davidson has one daughter and <u>for</u> <u>suns</u>.

     Ⓒ   Mrs. Davidson has one daughter and <u>four</u> <u>sons</u>.

     Ⓓ   Mrs. Davidson has one daughter and <u>four</u> <u>suns</u>.

Exercise 6

Write a sentence using each word.

 Each pair of words sound the same. Use the spelling of each word to work out its meaning. Then write a sentence using that meaning.

1 nose   *The ball hit Kenny in the nose.*

knows   *Nobody knows where the cat is hiding.*

2 sea   _____

see   _____

3 two   _____

too   _____

4 ad   _____

add   _____

5 so   _____

sew   _____

6 by   _____

bye   _____

Exercise 7

Write a word that describes what is shown in both pictures.

	star	

Exercise 8

Find the word that completes both sentences correctly. Write the missing words on the lines.

 The word that completes both sentences is spelled the same, but has a different meaning in each sentence.

1 The *bat* flew into the cave.

Joe hit the ball with his *bat*.

2 The _____ swam around on the pond.

Sam is tall. He had to _____ when he went through the door.

3 Nobody passed the test. It was too _____.

I fell off my bike onto the _____ ground.

4 The boat started to _____ from side to side.

Lola found a black _____ at the beach.

5 The dogs started to _____ when they saw each other.

The tree is covered with _____.

6 The desk was about a _____ long.

Kim often plays with the dog in her front _____.

Exercise 9

Find the word that is described by both clues. Write the word on the line.

 The two clues in each pair describe a word with the same spelling. Be sure to find a word that is a good answer for both clues.

1   You might do this when you say goodbye.   *wave*
    You might see one these at the beach.

2   This is a place where children play.   _____
    You would do this before getting out of a car.

3   You would put a shoe on this part of the body.   _____
    You could measure your height using this unit.

4   Two people in a ring might do this.   _____
    A present might be packed in this.

5   You might turn this off at night.   _____
    This word describes a feather.

6   This word is the opposite of left.   _____
    This word is the opposite of wrong.

7   You could travel on one of these.   _____
    You could do this to get better at something.

8   This word means "a type of something."   _____
    This word describes someone who is nice.

Exercise 10

Write two sentences using each word. Use a different meaning of the word in each sentence.

1 can   1. *We can go to the mall after school.*
               2. *I opened a can of soup.*

2 back   1. _____

               2. _____

3 trip   1. _____

               2. _____

4 play   1. _____

               2. _____

5 saw   1. _____

               2. _____

6 pick   1. _____

               2. _____

7 step   1. _____

               2. _____

Level 2

Exercises 11 to 20

Difficulty:

Building Your Vocabulary

As you complete the exercises, list any words you have trouble with below. Draw a picture or write down the meaning of each word.

Exercise 11

Circle the correct way to spell the name of the word shown by each picture.

	plain plane
	sun son
	tale tail
	shoo shoe
	rain rein

Exercise 12

Circle the correct spelling of each number.

for   four   ate   eight

one   won   too   two

Write a short paragraph that uses two or more of the words you circled.

_____

_____

_____

_____

Circle the correct spelling of each fruit or vegetable.

pare   pear   carrot   karat

bean   been   leak   leek

Write a short paragraph that uses two or more of the words you circled.

_____

_____

_____

_____

Exercise 13

Use the two given words to complete each sentence. Write the missing words on the lines.

1 fair   fare

It was not _____ for the bus _____ to cost so much.

2 shoo   shoe

I had to _____ the dog away before it took my _____.

3 road   rode

Emily _____ her bike along the side of the _____.

4 ad   add

The _____ said to _____ two dollars for postage.

5 hare   hair

The _____ had brown and white _____.

6 rose   rows

There was a _____ at the end of all the _____ of flowers.

Exercise 14

Circle the word in each sentence that is used incorrectly. Then rewrite the sentence using the correct word.

 One of the words in each sentence is spelled like another word that sounds the same. Find the word that has the wrong spelling.

1   My broken arm was very (soar.)

   My broken arm was very sore.

2   I cent a present to my aunt.

   _____

3   The tiles on the flaw look clean.

   _____

4   I was board by the long math class.

   _____

5   I court the ball with my right hand.

   _____

6   Jane tried to cell her old bike.

   _____

Exercise 15

Choose the best answer to each question.

1   Which sentence uses the underlined word correctly?

Ⓐ   Maggie bought the dress at a <u>sail</u>.

Ⓑ   Maggie bought the dress at a <u>sale</u>.

Ⓒ   Maggie bought the dress at a <u>seal</u>.

Ⓓ   Maggie bought the dress at a <u>sell</u>.

2   Which sentence uses the underlined word correctly?

Ⓐ   I would like to <u>rite</u> a book one day.

Ⓑ   I would like to <u>right</u> a book one day.

Ⓒ   I would like to <u>writ</u> a book one day.

Ⓓ   I would like to <u>write</u> a book one day.

3   Which sentence uses the underlined words correctly?

Ⓐ   The boys <u>road</u> down the river with a boat and two <u>oars</u>.

Ⓑ   The boys <u>road</u> down the river with a boat and two <u>ores</u>.

Ⓒ   The boys <u>rowed</u> down the river with a boat and two <u>oars</u>.

Ⓓ   The boys <u>rowed</u> down the river with a boat and two <u>ores</u>.

4   Which sentence uses the underlined words correctly?

Ⓐ   The <u>sole</u> of the shoe had been <u>warn</u> away.

Ⓑ   The <u>sole</u> of the shoe had been <u>worn</u> away.

Ⓒ   The <u>soul</u> of the shoe had been <u>warn</u> away.

Ⓓ   The <u>soul</u> of the shoe had been <u>worn</u> away.

Exercise 16

Write a sentence using each word.

 Each pair of words sound the same. Use the spelling of each word to work out its meaning. Then write a sentence using that meaning.

1 wood _____

   would _____

2 tea _____

   tee _____

3 hay _____

   hey _____

4 peace _____

   piece _____

5 in _____

   inn _____

6 we'd _____

   weed _____

Exercise 17

Find the word that describes what is shown in both pictures. Then write a sentence using the word. Circle the picture that uses the word in the same way as your sentence.

		Word: *block* Sentence: *The wall was put up to block the road.*
		Word: _____ Sentence: _____ _____
		Word: _____ Sentence: _____ _____
		Word: _____ Sentence: _____ _____
		Word: _____ Sentence: _____ _____

Exercise 18

Find the word that completes both sentences correctly. Write the missing words on the lines.

 The word that completes both sentences is spelled the same, but has a different meaning in each sentence.

1 Manny learned to _____ his shoelaces.

Liam put on his suit and _____.

2 Yuri does not feel _____ today.

The people get water from the _____.

3 Gemma's dog is very _____ to her.

The computer was too _____ to buy.

4 Michael gets _____ when people are late.

We could not _____ the high river.

5 I got a small _____ in the play.

I like to _____ my hair in the middle.

6 I used glue to _____ pictures in my scrapbook.

The dog picked up the _____ and brought it back.

Exercise 19

Find the word that is described by both clues. Write the word on the line.

 The two clues in each pair describe a word with the same spelling. Be sure to find a word that is a good answer for both clues.

1 A person who is angry might do this.
You do this when you pay for someone else.   *shout*

2 You could play the drums in one of these.
You might put one of these on your wrist.   _____

3 You might come this in a race.
This is a measure of time.   _____

4 A child might play with one of these.
A fallen tree could do this to a road.   _____

5 This word describes someone who is smart.
This word could describe a sunny day.   _____

6 You could run laps around one of these.
This word means "to follow."   _____

7 You might get this after paying for something.
People do this as they got older.   _____

8 A rock thrown into the water might do this.
You might find one of these in the kitchen.   _____

Exercise 20

Write two sentences using each word. Use a different meaning of the word in each sentence.

1 fair

1. *I had a lot of fun at the school fair.*
2. *The teams were picked in a fair way.*

2 left

1. _____

2. _____

3 wind

1. _____

2. _____

4 safe

1. _____

2. _____

5 hit

1. _____

2. _____

6 roll

1. _____

2. _____

7 lot

1. _____

2. _____

Level 3

Exercises 21 to 30

Difficulty:

Building Your Vocabulary

As you complete the exercises, list any words you have trouble with below. Draw a picture or write down the meaning of each word.

Exercise 21

Circle the correct way to spell the word represented by each picture. Then draw a picture or write the meaning of the other word in the empty column.

	weak week	*not strong*
	sail sale	
	cent scent	
	dear deer	
	hare hair	

Exercise 22

Circle the correct spelling of each part of the body.

feat   feet   nose   knows

hair   heir   waste   waist

ear   ere   heal   heel

nee   knee   toe   tow

scull   skull   brows   browse

Write a short paragraph that uses two or more of the words you circled.

_____

_____

_____

_____

Circle the correct spelling of each type of plant or tree.

fir   fur   beach   beech

rose   rows   cedar   seeder

Exercise 23

Use the two given words to complete each sentence. Write the missing words on the lines.

1 saw   soar

I _____ the bird _____ high up into the sky.

2 seen   scene

I had never _____ the movie _____ before.

3 threw   through

I_____ the ball _____ the window.

4 fowl   foul

The smell of the_____ was quite _____.

Write a sentence that uses both of the words given below.

5 made   maid

_____

6 ate   eight

_____

Exercise 24

Circle the word in each sentence that is used incorrectly. Then write a sentence that uses the word you circled correctly.

 Find the word in each sentence that is spelled like another word that sounds the same. Then write a sentence that uses the correct meaning of the word you circled.

1 I do not like to (waist) any money.

I put the belt around my waist.

2 Alison filled the pale with water.

_____

3 The window pain has a small crack in it.

_____

4 The manager decided to higher someone new.

_____

5 There was a sale on, but not many things were cheep.

_____

6 I was scared when I first heard the lion raw.

_____

Exercise 25

Choose the best answer to each question.

1   Which sentence uses the underlined word correctly?

   Ⓐ   The fisherman put <u>bait</u> on the end of his hook.

   Ⓑ   The fisherman put <u>bate</u> on the end of his hook.

   Ⓒ   The fisherman put <u>beat</u> on the end of his hook.

   Ⓓ   The fisherman put <u>beet</u> on the end of his hook.

2   Which sentence uses the underlined word correctly?

   Ⓐ   It is rude to <u>stair</u> at people.

   Ⓑ   It is rude to <u>stare</u> at people.

   Ⓒ   It is rude to <u>store</u> at people.

   Ⓓ   It is rude to <u>steer</u> at people.

3   Which sentence uses the underlined words correctly?

   Ⓐ   A <u>doe</u> is a female <u>dear</u>.

   Ⓑ   A <u>doe</u> is a female <u>deer</u>.

   Ⓒ   A <u>dough</u> is a female <u>dear</u>.

   Ⓓ   A <u>dough</u> is a female <u>deer</u>.

4   Which sentence uses the underlined words correctly?

   Ⓐ   James often <u>wares</u> a hat because he is <u>bald</u>.

   Ⓑ   James often <u>wares</u> a hat because he is <u>bawled</u>.

   Ⓒ   James often <u>wears</u> a hat because he is <u>bald</u>.

   Ⓓ   James often <u>wears</u> a hat because he is <u>bawled</u>.

Exercise 26

Write a sentence using each word.

 Each pair of words sound the same. Use the spelling of each word to work out its meaning. Then write a sentence using that meaning.

1 days _____

    daze _____

2 wax _____

    whacks _____

3 side _____

    sighed _____

4 team _____

    teem _____

5 who's _____

    whose _____

6 its _____

    it's _____

Exercise 27

Write a word that describes what is shown in both pictures.

_____	*line*	

Exercise 28

Find the word that completes both sentences correctly. Write the missing words on the lines.

1 There were an _even_ number of students.

   I was so tired I couldn't _even_ keep my eyes open.

2 Doreen brushed her teeth and washed her _____.

   Joel felt bad and could not _____ his sister.

3 I bought new shorts and a new _____.

   I put a bar of soap on _____ of the towels.

4 The team's loss was a _____ to their chances of making the finals.

   James tried to _____ out all the candles.

5 I decided to _____ my dirty clothes.

   I was given two dimes and two nickels as _____.

6 We found a lovely _____ for our picnic.

   I could not _____ my friend in the crowd.

Exercise 29

Find the word that matches both meanings. Then write a sentence using each meaning of the word.

1 one of the four seasons   *fall*
    the act of moving down

    1. *The trees look lovely during the fall.*
    2. *The snow began to fall.*

2 to call or phone   _____
    a band worn on the finger

    1. _____

    2. _____

3 having little money   _____
    having little skill

    1. _____

    2. _____

4 to look at or view   _____
    an object worn to tell the time

    1. _____

    2. _____

Exercise 30

Describe two different meanings for each word.

1 trunk   1. *a large case*
             2. *the middle part of a tree*

2 plant   1. _____

             2. _____

3 round   1. _____

             2. _____

4 still   1. _____

             2. _____

5 flash   1. _____

             2. _____

6 lock   1. _____

             2. _____

7 table   1. _____

             2. _____

Level 4

Exercises 31 to 40

Difficulty:

Building Your Vocabulary

As you complete the exercises, list any words you have trouble with below. Draw a picture or write down the meaning of each word.

Exercise 31

Circle the correct way to spell the word represented by each picture. Then draw a picture or write the meaning of the other word in the empty column.

	great grate	
	brake break	
	beach beech	
	flower flour	
	pitcher picture	

Exercise 32

Circle the two words in each list that sound the same. Then write a sentence using one of the words you circled.

 Read each list of words out loud. Focus on the sound of each word.

1 dry   die   dye   doe

_____

2 stay   stack   stake   steak

_____

3 stir   stair   stare   star

_____

4 stray   story   storey   sorry

_____

5 mode   mood   mowed   moored

_____

6 kite   knit   knight   night

_____

Exercise 33

Use the two given words to complete each sentence. Write the missing words on the lines.

1 warn   worn

I forgot to_____ Mandy that she should have _____ a coat.

2 wait   weight

I could not _____ to find out the puppy's _____.

3 hear   here

From all the way back _____, it is very hard to _____.

4 hall   haul

We had to_____ the desk all the way along the _____.

Write a sentence that uses both of the words given below.

5 herd   heard

_____

6 we're   where

_____

Exercise 34

Circle the word in each sentence that is used incorrectly. Then write a sentence that uses the word you circled correctly.

 Find the word in each sentence that is spelled like another word that sounds the same. Then write a sentence that uses the correct meaning of the word you circled.

1   Frank watched a bird chew on a (read.)

I am going to relax and read my book.

2   Malik picked a flour from the garden and gave it to his wife.

_____

3   It did not seam like the plumber knew what he was doing.

_____

4   Rosita tried to sow a new dress to give to her aunt.

_____

5   I bought an old pair of gloves for two dollars and fifty sense.

_____

6   I wood not have gone out if I knew it was going to rain all day.

_____

Exercise 35

Choose the best answer to each question.

1   Which sentence uses the underlined word correctly?

    Ⓐ   The town <u>mar</u> made a speech.

    Ⓑ   The town <u>mare</u> made a speech.

    Ⓒ   The town <u>mere</u> made a speech.

    Ⓓ   The town <u>mayor</u> made a speech.

2   Which sentence uses the underlined words correctly?

    Ⓐ   The farmer <u>led</u> the <u>horse</u> up the hill.

    Ⓑ   The farmer <u>led</u> the <u>hoarse</u> up the hill.

    Ⓒ   The farmer <u>lead</u> the <u>horse</u> up the hill.

    Ⓓ   The farmer <u>lead</u> the <u>hoarse</u> up the hill.

3   Which word does NOT sound the same as the other three words?

    Ⓐ   there   Ⓒ   tear

    Ⓑ   they're   Ⓓ   their

4   Which word does NOT sound the same as the other three words?

    Ⓐ   war   Ⓒ   wear

    Ⓑ   ware   Ⓓ   where

5   Which word does NOT sound the same as the other three words?

    Ⓐ   saw   Ⓒ   so

    Ⓑ   sew   Ⓓ   sow

Exercise 36

For each word given, write another word that sounds the same. Then explain what the word means.

 Say the word out loud. Then think of another word that sounds the same, but has a different spelling.

1 watt   a unit that gives a measure of power

     what   *a word used to ask a question*

2 banned   not allowed to

_____   _____

3 urn   a type of vase

_____   _____

4 phew   a word used to show relief or surprise

_____   _____

5 spar   to box lightly

_____   _____

6 loan   to borrow money

_____   _____

Exercise 37

Find the word that describes what is represented by both pictures. Then write a sentence using the word. Circle the picture that uses the word in the same way as your sentence.

		Word: _____ Sentence: _____ _____
		Word: _____ Sentence: _____ _____
		Word: _____ Sentence: _____ _____
		Word: _____ Sentence: _____ _____
		Word: _____ Sentence: _____ _____

Exercise 38

Find the word that completes both sentences correctly. Write the missing words on the lines.

 The word that completes both sentences is spelled the same, but has a different meaning in each sentence.

1 I asked my mother to _____ my shirt.

The _____ nail began to rust.

2 The underground _____ was dark and damp.

It rained so hard I thought the roof might _____ in.

3 I do not _____ helping my sister with her homework.

Puzzles can make you smarter and improve your_____.

4 It is important to learn to_____ stress.

Sean carried the suitcase by its _____.

5 Fiona was upset when she dropped her phone and _____ it.

After spending his last penny, Jayden was _____.

6 The basketball team cheered when Jerry made the winning _____.

The rocket was _____ into space.

Exercise 39

Find the word that is described by both clues. Write the word on the line.

1 This is another name for a bird's beak.   *bill*
   You might be given one after eating a meal.

2 You might eat your dinner off one of these.   _____
   You might run over one when playing baseball.

3 This is another name for a faucet.   _____
   You do this when you knock lightly.

4 A vase might do this if you drop it.   _____
   You might need one during a long test.

5 You might find treasure inside this.   _____
   You might put a medal on this part of the body.

6 You might write a message on one of these.   _____
   You might play one of these on the piano.

7 You would see one of these on a runway.   _____
   This word describes a smaller version of an object.

8 This unit is used to measure length.   _____
   This word means to move forward slowly.

Exercise 40

Write two sentences using each word. Use a different meaning of the word in each sentence.

1 beat   1. _____

2. _____

2 bow   1. _____

2. _____

3 act   1. _____

2. _____

4 class   1. _____

2. _____

5 cool   1. _____

2. _____

6 free   1. _____

2. _____

Level 5

Exercises 41 to 50

Difficulty: ⭐⭐☆

Building Your Vocabulary

As you complete the exercises, list any words you have trouble with below. Draw a picture or write down the meaning of each word.

Exercise 41

Circle the correct way to spell the word represented by each picture.

	claws clause
	night knight
	genes jeans
	miner minor
	lynx links

Exercise 42

Circle the correct spelling of each animal.

bare	bear		horse	hoarse
flea	flee		wail	whale
hair	hare		mite	might
be	bee		boar	bore
you	ewe		dear	deer
toad	toed		gnu	knew
fowl	foul		tern	turn

Write a short paragraph that uses three or more of the words you circled.

_____

_____

_____

_____

Exercise 43

Use the two given words to complete each sentence. Write the missing words on the lines.

1 strait   straight

The boat sailed_____ along the _____.

2 fax   facts

The _____ contains all the _____ you'll need to know.

3 tents   tense

I felt _____ about getting the_____ up in time.

4 throne   thrown

The king's _____ was _____ away.

Write a sentence that uses both of the words given below.

5 ball   bawl

_____

6 they're   their

_____

Exercise 44

Circle the word in each sentence that is used incorrectly. Then write a sentence that uses the word you circled correctly.

1   Johanna asked her boss for a (rays.)

The rays of the sun shone down on the pond.

2   Rats have long teeth that allow them to nor on things like wood.

_____

3   Todd was given a meddle for helping to clean up his town.

_____

4   The seem at the bottom of the dress was starting to come undone.

_____

5   The farmer had to sew all the seeds before it became too warm.

_____

6   Rachel tried to peak through the door to see what was going on.

_____

Exercise 45

Choose the best answer to each question.

1   Which sentence uses the underlined word correctly?

    Ⓐ   I don't think <u>hell</u> win the race.

    Ⓑ   I don't think <u>he'll</u> win the race.

    Ⓒ   I don't think <u>heal</u> win the race.

    Ⓓ   I don't think <u>heel</u> win the race.

2   Which sentence uses the underlined words correctly?

    Ⓐ   The teacher gave a <u>lessen</u> on how to <u>right</u>.

    Ⓑ   The teacher gave a <u>lessen</u> on how to <u>write</u>.

    Ⓒ   The teacher gave a <u>lesson</u> on how to <u>right</u>.

    Ⓓ   The teacher gave a <u>lesson</u> on how to <u>write</u>.

3   Which word does NOT sound the same as the other three words?

    Ⓐ   to   Ⓒ   two

    Ⓑ   toe   Ⓓ   too

4   Which word does NOT sound the same as the other three words?

    Ⓐ   toad   Ⓒ   toed

    Ⓑ   towed   Ⓓ   tread

5   Which word does NOT sound the same as the other three words?

    Ⓐ   met   Ⓒ   meet

    Ⓑ   meat   Ⓓ   mete

Exercise 46

For each word given, write another word that sounds the same and give the meaning of the word.

1 nay   another way of saying no

   neigh   *the sound a horse makes*

2 moor   an area of land without trees

_____   _____

3 tern   a type of bird

_____   _____

4 reel   a winder on a fishing rod

_____   _____

5 wee   very small

_____   _____

6 altar   a stand with a flat top

_____   _____

Exercise 47

Find the word that describes what is represented by both pictures.

Exercise 48

Find the word that completes both sentences correctly. Write the missing words on the lines.

 The word that completes both sentences is spelled the same, but has a different meaning in each sentence.

1 We waited _____ for the bus.

The _____ of all my friends are about the same.

2 With just one lap to go, Jeremy was in the _____.

Penny knew the most, so she wanted to _____ the team.

3 I entered the _____ and pressed the button for the tenth floor.

The huge rock was far too heavy to _____.

4 I bought about one _____ of bananas.

I had to _____ the metal with a hammer to make it flat.

5 The chocolate cake was _____ and delicious.

Phillip became _____ when he won money on a game show.

6 The elephants roamed about on the wide_____.

I decided to wear a _____ tie instead of one with a pattern.

Exercise 49

Find the word that matches both meanings. Then write a sentence using each meaning of the word.

1 to rescue someone   _____
   to set aside money

   1. _____

   2. _____

2 able to be seen through   _____
   free from clouds

   1. _____

   2. _____

3 to pass out   _____
   dim or hard to see

   1. _____

   2. _____

4 a wood or metal pole   _____
   to send something in the mail

   1. _____

   2. _____

Exercise 50

Describe two different meanings for each word.

1 match   1. *to look the same*
              2. *an item used to make fire*

2 fan   1. _____

          2. _____

3 club   1. _____

          2. _____

4 dash 1. _____

          2. _____

5 skip   1. _____

          2. _____

6 star   1. _____

          2. _____

7 spring 1. _____

          2. _____

Level 6

Exercises 51 to 60

Difficulty:

Building Your Vocabulary

As you complete the exercises, list any words you have trouble with below. Draw a picture or write down the meaning of each word.

Exercise 51

Circle the correct way to spell the word represented by each picture.

	isle aisle
	muscle mussel
	quarts quartz
	throne thrown
	yoke yolk

Exercise 52

Circle the two words in each list that sound the same. Then write a sentence using one of the words you circled.

1   bead   bread   bred   bed

_____

2   hail   hale   heel   hole

_____

3   sent   sheen   scene   scent

_____

4   piece   peace   pace   pass

_____

5   sit   seat   sight   site

_____

6   hour   heir   our   owe

_____

Exercise 53

Use the two given words to complete each sentence. Write the missing words on the lines.

1 fore   four

The golfer had to yell _____ at least _____ times.

2 main   mane

The _____ thing I noticed about the lion was its _____.

3 might   mite

Chloe _____ have been bitten by a _____.

4 paws   pause

After a short _____ the cat continued to lick its _____.

Write a sentence that uses both of the words given below.

5 coarse   course

_____

6 plain   plane

_____

Exercise 54

For each sentence, cross out the word that is spelled incorrectly and write the correct word. Write a sentence that uses the word you crossed out correctly.

course

1 Ellen wanted to learn to write poems, so she took a ~~coarse~~.

The sandpaper was very coarse.

2 The workers spent days trying to find the sauce of the problem.

_____

3 Robin was looking forward to hearing the school belle ring.

_____

4 The most popular desert at the diner was the apple tart.

_____

5 Sammy was upset when she saw there was a whole in her sweater.

_____

6 Janet put on her shoes and then tide the laces.

_____

Exercise 55

Choose the best answer to each question.

1   Which sentence uses the underlined word correctly?

Ⓒ   The baby began to <u>wail</u> when its dummy was taken.

Ⓓ   The baby began to <u>wale</u> when its dummy was taken.

Ⓔ   The baby began to <u>whale</u> when its dummy was taken.

Ⓕ   The baby began to <u>wheel</u> when its dummy was taken.

2   Which sentence uses the underlined words correctly?

Ⓒ   Nobody was <u>aloud</u> to swim in the castle's <u>moat</u>.

Ⓓ   Nobody was <u>aloud</u> to swim in the castle's <u>mote</u>.

Ⓔ   Nobody was <u>allowed</u> to swim in the castle's <u>moat</u>.

Ⓕ   Nobody was <u>allowed</u> to swim in the castle's <u>mote</u>.

3   Which word does NOT sound the same as the other three words?

Ⓒ   cite   Ⓔ   sit

Ⓓ   site   Ⓕ   sight

4   Which word does NOT sound the same as the other three words?

Ⓒ   pair   Ⓔ   peer

Ⓓ   pear   Ⓕ   pare

5   Which word does NOT sound the same as the other three words?

Ⓒ   flu   Ⓔ   flue

Ⓓ   fly   Ⓕ   flew

Exercise 56

Write a sentence using each word.

 Each pair of words sound the same. Use the spelling of each word to work out its meaning. Then write a sentence using that meaning.

1 crews   1. _____

    cruise   2. _____

2 shear   1. _____

    sheer   2. _____

3 ceiling   1. _____

    sealing   2. _____

4 grays   1. _____

    graze   2. _____

5 pleas   1. _____

    please   2. _____

6 paced   1. _____

    paste   2. _____

Exercise 57

Find the word that completes both sentences correctly. Write the missing words on the lines.

1 We arrived at school _____ in time.

The decision the coach made was fair and _____.

2 The _____ of birds flew a long way together.

The people began to _____ to the new store.

3 There were many people in the line, so it was a _____ wait.

Portia missed Miami and would often _____ to be back there.

4 I decided to have one _____ of vanilla ice cream.

The reporter was always looking for a new _____.

5 Georgina Gutierrez sometimes forgets how to _____ her own name.

The witches tried to cast a _____ to turn Jenny into a toad.

6 I wanted the letter to be neat, so I decided to _____ it.

Fiona's favorite _____ of pie is apple pie.

Exercise 58

For each question, choose the word that best completes both phrases.

 The correct answer completes both phrases instead of just one.

1 knife and _____   _____ in the road

    Ⓐ spoon   Ⓑ fork   Ⓒ bend   Ⓓ break

2 speeding _____   _____ weather

    Ⓐ car   Ⓑ nice   Ⓒ hot   Ⓓ fine

3 talk to the _____   _____ the button

    Ⓐ friend   Ⓑ check   Ⓒ press   Ⓓ camera

4 _____ a photo   _____ for the crime

    Ⓐ sold   Ⓑ took   Ⓒ framed   Ⓓ worried

5 block of _____   _____ a plane

    Ⓐ land   Ⓑ houses   Ⓒ board   Ⓓ fly

6 read a street _____   _____ a check

    Ⓐ flyer   Ⓑ sign   Ⓒ write   Ⓓ cash

Exercise 59

Describe two different meanings for each word.

1 lean   1. *to bend to the side*
              2. *thin or skinny*

2 close   1. _____

              2. _____

3 net   1. _____

              2. _____

4 shower 1. _____

              2. _____

5 produce 1. _____

              2. _____

6 peer   1. _____

              2. _____

7 simple 1. _____

              2. _____

Exercise 60

Nouns are words that name people, places, things, or ideas. Verbs are words that state an action. Some words can be used as both nouns and verbs. For each word listed, write one sentence using the word as a noun and one sentence using the word as a verb.

1 drink   Noun: *I am going to have a drink of juice.*
              Verb: *I like to drink warm milk.*

2 walk   Noun: _____

            Verb: _____

3 mail   Noun: _____

            Verb: _____

4 dress   Noun: _____

            Verb: _____

5 mop   Noun: _____

            Verb: _____

6 drive   Noun: _____

            Verb: _____

Level 7

Exercises 61 to 70

Difficulty: ★★☆

Building Your Vocabulary

As you complete the exercises, list any words you have trouble with below. Draw a picture or write down the meaning of each word.

Exercise 61

Circle the correct way to spell the word represented by each picture. Then write a sentence using the word you circled.

	knot not	_____ _____
	flee flea	_____ _____
	which witch	_____ _____
	way weigh	_____ _____
	hail hale	_____ _____
	plum plumb	_____ _____

Exercise 62

Circle the correct spelling of each word that names a food.

meat	meet	bred	bread
bury	berry	beat	beet
stake	steak	cereal	serial
maze	maize	doe	dough
pi	pie	role	roll
time	thyme	Sunday	sundae
jam	jamb	currant	current

Write a short paragraph that uses three or more of the words you circled.

_____

_____

_____

_____

_____

Exercise 63

Use the two given words to complete each sentence. Write the missing words on the lines.

1 guest   guessed

I _____ that the secret _____ was my aunt.

2 miner   minor

The gold_____ only had a _____ injury.

3 weather whether

I did not know_____ the _____ would be nice.

4 creak   creek

The bridge crossing the _____ began to _____.

Write a sentence that uses both of the words given below.

5 rode   road

_____

6 write   right

_____

Exercise 64

For each sentence, cross out the word that is spelled incorrectly and write the correct word. Write a sentence that uses the word you crossed out correctly.

idol

1 An ~~idle~~ is somebody that you look up to and admire.

_____

2 We whirr going to bake a cake, but we could not find any eggs.

_____

3 If ewe are unsure what to do, just ask somebody for help.

_____

4 I drew a pretty boarder around the outside of the page.

_____

5 I want to buy the computer, but I have to ask the cellar some questions first.

_____

6 A poem that gives praise to something is called an owed.

_____

Exercise 65

Choose the best answer to each question.

1   Which sentence uses the underlined words correctly?

    Ⓐ   The small <u>plain</u> was stored in the <u>hangar</u>.

    Ⓑ   The small <u>plain</u> was stored in the <u>hanger</u>.

    Ⓒ   The small <u>plane</u> was stored in the <u>hangar</u>.

    Ⓓ   The small <u>plane</u> was stored in the <u>hanger</u>.

2   Which sentence uses the underlined words correctly?

    Ⓐ   The hotel <u>suite</u> offered a <u>grate</u> view.

    Ⓑ   The hotel <u>suite</u> offered a <u>great</u> view.

    Ⓒ   The hotel <u>sweet</u> offered a <u>grate</u> view.

    Ⓓ   The hotel <u>sweet</u> offered a <u>great</u> view.

3   Which word does NOT sound the same as the other three words?

    Ⓐ   buy   Ⓒ   buoy

    Ⓑ   by   Ⓓ   bye

4   Which word does NOT sound the same as the other three words?

    Ⓐ   awe   Ⓒ   or

    Ⓑ   oar   Ⓓ   are

5   Which word does NOT sound the same as the other three words?

    Ⓐ   vane   Ⓒ   vain

    Ⓑ   vine   Ⓓ   vein

Exercise 66

Write a sentence using each word. Be sure to use the correct meaning of the word in the sentence.

1 prince _____

prints _____

2 bazaar _____

bizarre _____

3 colonel _____

kernel _____

4 symbol _____

cymbal _____

5 morning _____

mourning _____

6 faze _____

phase _____

Exercise 67

Find the word that describes what is represented by both pictures. Then write a sentence using the word. Circle the picture that uses the word in the same way as your sentence.

		Word: _____ Sentence: _____ _____
		Word: _____ Sentence: _____ _____
		Word: _____ Sentence: _____ _____
		Word: _____ Sentence: _____ _____
		Word: _____ Sentence: _____ _____

Exercise 68

Find the word that completes both sentences correctly. Write the missing words on the lines.

1 We used a microscope to look at the _____ of plants.

   The _____ of the old prison we toured were very small.

2 I wanted to get _____, so I started running each morning.

   The key was too large to _____ in the lock.

3 The band members have a _____ session every Friday.

   The huge traffic _____ made many people late for work.

4 We had never won a game before, so our win was a huge _____.

   The toaster gave Bianca an electric _____.

5 The author had to _____ hundreds of books for her fans.

   The road _____ warned drivers to be careful of deer.

6 Quentin had to use a lot of _____ to open the jar.

   Layla tried to _____ the horse to move, but it stayed still.

Exercise 69

Find the word that is described by both clues. Write the word on the line.

1   You might wear one if you broke your arm.   _____
    This word describes all the people in a play.

2   A rooster does this to make noise.   _____
    This is a type of black bird.

3   This is a small round item used to play games.   _____
    This is a type of rock often used to make tiles.

4   You might chew on this.   _____
    This is the part of the mouth that holds the teeth.

5   This pattern can often be seen on tablecloths.   _____
    You might be paid with one of these.

6   You might go to one of these to get money.   _____
    This can form when sand piles up at the side of a river.

7   You find these in the roofs of buildings.   _____
    These are produced when torches are turned on.

8   This is another word for a company.   _____
    This is what dry soil might feel like.

Exercise 70

Write two sentences using each word. Use a different meaning of the word in each sentence.

1 sweet

1. _____

2. _____

2 cool

1. _____

2. _____

3 bold

1. _____

2. _____

4 felt

1. _____

2. _____

5 race

1. _____

2. _____

6 print

1. _____

2. _____

Level 8

Exercises 71 to 80

Difficulty:

Building Your Vocabulary

As you complete the exercises, list any words you have trouble with below. Draw a picture or write down the meaning of each word.

Exercise 71

Circle the correct way to spell the word represented by each picture. Then write a sentence using the word you circled.

	ad add	
	wail whale	
	wave waive	
	stair stare	
	bite byte	
	pole poll	

Exercise 72

Circle the two words in each list that sound the same. Then write a sentence explaining the meaning of each word you circled.

1 dare   (deer)   dire   (dear)

     1. A deer is a type of animal.
     2. Something that is dear costs a lot.

2 warp   wrap   rap   race

    1. _____

    2. _____

3 rise   wise   raise   rays

    1. _____

    2. _____

4 flea   flue   flee   fly

    1. _____

    2. _____

5 flour   floor   flare   flaw

    1. _____

    2. _____

Exercise 73

Use the two given words to complete each sentence. Write the missing words on the lines.

1 weak   week

I felt sick and _____ for most of last_____.

2 leak   leek

The potato and _____ soup began to _____ everywhere.

3 maze   maize

The paths through the field of_____ were like a _____.

4 find   fined

Craig was upset to _____ he had been _____ for speeding.

Write a sentence that uses both of the words given below.

5 your   you're

_____

6 wood   would

_____

Exercise 74

Circle the word in each sentence that is used incorrectly. Then write a sentence that uses the word you circled correctly.

 One of the words in each sentence is spelled like another word that sounds the same. Find the word that has the wrong spelling.

1 The dancers world their partners around very fast.

_____

2 Both men drew their swords and the dual began.

_____

3 The barren and his wife were part of the royal family.

_____

4 Mr. Browning saved money so he could pay his tacks.

_____

5 Joel knew he would have to take chances and be boulder to succeed.

_____

6 The naughty dog choose on any shoes it finds lying around.

_____

Exercise 75

Choose the best answer to each question.

1. Which sentence uses the underlined word correctly?

    Ⓐ   Mark has already <u>groan</u> another two inches taller this year.

    Ⓑ   Mark has already <u>grown</u> another two inches taller this year.

    Ⓒ   Mark has already <u>grain</u> another two inches taller this year.

    Ⓓ   Mark has already <u>grand</u> another two inches taller this year.

2. Which sentence uses the underlined words correctly?

    Ⓐ   There was only one <u>peace</u> of pumpkin <u>pi</u> left.

    Ⓑ   There was only one <u>peace</u> of pumpkin <u>pie</u> left.

    Ⓒ   There was only one <u>piece</u> of pumpkin <u>pi</u> left.

    Ⓓ   There was only one <u>piece</u> of pumpkin <u>pie</u> left.

3. Which word does NOT sound the same as the other three words?

    Ⓐ   for   Ⓑ   fore

    Ⓒ   fur   Ⓓ   four

4. Which word does NOT sound the same as the other three words?

    Ⓐ   seas   Ⓒ   size

    Ⓑ   sees   Ⓓ   seize

5. Which word does NOT sound the same as the other three words?

    Ⓐ   ring   Ⓒ   reign

    Ⓑ   rain   Ⓓ   rein

Exercise 76

Write a sentence using each word. Be sure to use the correct meaning of the word in the sentence.

1 scull _____

skull _____

2 rapped _____

wrapped _____

3 based _____

baste _____

4 brood _____

brewed _____

5 chili _____

chilly _____

6 mince _____

mints _____

Exercise 77

Find the word that completes both sentences correctly. Write the missing words on the lines. Then write a new sentence that used the word a third way.

1   The tiger looked like it was about to *spring*.

    The water in the *spring* sometimes freezes in winter.

    The flowers began to bloom in spring.

2   I used the _____ on the map to work out the distance.

    I used a _____ to find the weight of my dog.

    _____

3   Jennifer had to _____ the baby to stop her from crying.

    Oliver most likes playing _____ music on his guitar.

    _____

4   There were a lot of people waiting in _____ at the store.

    A ruler is a good tool to use when drawing a straight _____.

    _____

5   The weather report said that Tuesday will be _____.

    My father got a _____ because he was driving too fast.

    _____

Exercise 78

For each question, choose the word that best completes both phrases.

 Make sure the answer you choose completes both phrases well.

1 join the _____   golf _____

   Ⓐ party   Ⓑ club   Ⓒ cart   Ⓓ dots

2 swim in the _____   _____ the money together

   Ⓐ pond   Ⓑ join   Ⓒ pool   Ⓓ sea

3 _____ up the hill   _____ your memory

   Ⓐ climb   Ⓑ jog   Ⓒ test   Ⓓ improve

4 _____ a cab   rain and _____

   Ⓐ stop   Ⓑ drive   Ⓒ hail   Ⓓ snow

5 puffs and _____   shirt and _____

   Ⓐ pants   Ⓑ shoes   Ⓒ tie   Ⓓ huffs

6 break the _____   _____ a hit song

   Ⓐ vase   Ⓑ chain   Ⓒ sing   Ⓓ record

Exercise 79

Write two sentences using each word. Use a different meaning of the word in each sentence.

1 grave   1. _____

           2. _____

2 drag   1. _____

           2. _____

3 coast   1. _____

           2. _____

4 cart   1. _____

           2. _____

5 pepper   1. _____

           2. _____

6 flare   1. _____

           2. _____

Exercise 80

Nouns are words that name people, places, things, or ideas. Verbs are words that state an action. Some words can be used as both nouns and verbs. For each word listed, write one sentence using the word as a noun and one sentence using the word as a verb.

1 vote   Noun: *The first vote read out was for Kim.*
            Verb: *I decided to vote James for class president.*

2 knock   Noun: _____

            Verb: _____

3 trap   Noun: _____

            Verb: _____

4 guess   Noun: _____

            Verb: _____

5 nurse   Noun: _____

            Verb: _____

6 water   Noun: _____

            Verb: _____

Level 9

Exercises 81 to 90

Difficulty: ★★★

Building Your Vocabulary

As you complete the exercises, list any words you have trouble with below. Draw a picture or write down the meaning of each word.

Exercise 81

Circle the correct way to spell the word represented by each picture. Then write a sentence using the word you circled.

Picture	Word	Sentence
	moose / mousse	_____ _____
	fairy / ferry	_____ _____
	urn / earn	_____ _____
	pail / pale	_____ _____
	herd / heard	_____ _____
	real / reel	_____ _____

Exercise 82

Circle the correct spelling of the word in each pair that names a person.

aren't   aunt   guest   guessed

nun   none   hair   heir

bow   beau   boy   buoy

bell   belle   made   maid

which   witch   prince   prints

son   sun   night   knight

kernel   colonel   juggler   jugular

profit   prophet   idol   idle

Write a short paragraph that uses three or more of the words you circled.

_____

_____

_____

_____

Exercise 83

Use the two given words to complete each sentence. Write the missing words on the lines.

1 cue   queue

Maxwell joined the_____ right on _____.

2 dew   due

We are _____ for a cold morning with _____.

3 feat   feet

The motorcycle jumping 300 _____ was an amazing _____.

4 buries   berries

The squirrel often _____ nuts and _____.

Write a sentence that uses both of the words given below.

5 sure   shore

_____

6 we'll   wheel

_____

Exercise 84

For each sentence, cross out the word that is spelled incorrectly and write the correct word. Write a sentence that uses the word you crossed out correctly.

1 The ferry will be leaving at noon from the ~~key~~. *quay*

You need the right key to open this door.

2 The present is wrapped nicely and has a lovely red beau on it.

_____

3 There are eight more buoys than girls in the school choir.

_____

4 Harrison was such a bad driver that his car had many dense in it.

_____

5 The tablecloth is not made well and phrase too easily.

_____

6 Tessa was tired after running several lapse of the running track.

_____

Exercise 85

Choose the best answer to each question.

1   Which sentence uses the underlined words correctly?

    Ⓐ   Nikolai always takes <u>pride</u> in having good <u>manors</u>.

    Ⓑ   Nikolai always takes <u>pride</u> in having good <u>manners</u>.

    Ⓒ   Nikolai always takes <u>pried</u> in having good <u>manors</u>.

    Ⓓ   Nikolai always takes <u>pried</u> in having good <u>manners</u>.

2   Which sentence uses the underlined words correctly?

    Ⓐ   The <u>revue</u> of the book said the <u>forward</u> was good.

    Ⓑ   The <u>revue</u> of the book said the <u>foreword</u> was good.

    Ⓒ   The <u>review</u> of the book said the <u>forward</u> was good.

    Ⓓ   The <u>review</u> of the book said the <u>foreword</u> was good.

3   Which word does NOT sound the same as the other three words?

    Ⓐ   saw   Ⓒ   sore

    Ⓑ   soar   Ⓓ   sir

4   Which word does NOT sound the same as the other three words?

    Ⓐ   why   Ⓒ   whey

    Ⓑ   way   Ⓓ   weigh

5   Which word does NOT sound the same as the other three words?

    Ⓐ   holy   Ⓒ   holey

    Ⓑ   holly   Ⓓ   wholly

Exercise 86

For each word given, write another word that sounds the same and give a meaning of the word.

1 roe   the eggs of fish

    row   *using oars to make a boat move*

2 joule   a unit that measures energy

_____   _____

3 larva   a young form of an insect

_____   _____

4 tuber   part of the root of a plant

_____   _____

5 tiers   layers placed on top of each other

_____   _____

6 sword   a weapon with a long blade

_____   _____

7 fir   a type of evergreen tree

_____   _____

Exercise 87

Find the word that describes what is represented by both pictures. Then write a sentence using the word. Circle the picture that uses the word in the same way as your sentence.

		Word: _____ Sentence: _____ _____
		Word: _____ Sentence: _____ _____
		Word: _____ Sentence: _____ _____
		Word: _____ Sentence: _____ _____
		Word: _____ Sentence: _____ _____

Exercise 88

For each question, choose the word that best completes both phrases.

1 even and _____   _____ behavior

   Ⓐ odd   Ⓑ low   © strange   Ⓓ rough

2 kick a field _____   plan to reach a _____

   Ⓐ ball   Ⓑ purpose   © goal   Ⓓ point

3 _____ of the foot   the _____ survivor

   Ⓐ bottom   Ⓑ sole   © only   Ⓓ heel

4 _____ your hands   loud _____ of thunder

   Ⓐ wash   Ⓑ dry   © storm   Ⓓ clap

5 have a _____ call   _____ the door

   Ⓐ close   Ⓑ phone   © slam   Ⓓ long

6 _____ back and forth   run at your own _____

   Ⓐ jump   Ⓑ game   © pace   Ⓓ look

Exercise 89

Find the word that matches both meanings. Then write a sentence using each meaning of the word.

 Some of the words are spelled the same, but sound different.

1 a measure of time   _____
   very small

   1. _____

   2. _____

2 able to wait without being annoyed   _____
   someone receiving treatment from a doctor

   1. _____

   2. _____

3 an animal kept at home   _____
   someone who is a favorite

   1. _____

   2. _____

4 jumped off a platform into the water   _____
   a type of bird that often represents peace

   1. _____

   2. _____

Exercise 90

Describe two or three different meanings for each word.

1 tip   1. _____

           2. _____

2 place   1. _____

           2. _____

           3. _____

3 dart   1. _____

           2. _____

4 drill   1. _____

           2. _____

5 jar   1. _____

           2. _____

6 tear   1. _____

           2. _____

           3. _____

Level 10

Exercises 91 to 101

Difficulty:

Building Your Vocabulary

As you complete the exercises, list any words you have trouble with below. Draw a picture or write down the meaning of each word.

Exercise 91

Circle the correct way to spell the word represented by each picture. Then write a sentence using the word you circled.

	peal / peel	_____
	suite / sweet	_____
	root / route	_____
	pedal / peddle	_____
	court / caught	_____
	maze / maize	_____

Exercise 92

Circle the two words in each list that sound the same. Then write a sentence explaining the meaning of each word you circled.

1 lean   lone   loan   loon

    1. _____

    2. _____

2 steal   steel   stale   stall

    1. _____

    2. _____

3 bet   beet   bat   beat

    1. _____

    2. _____

4 seer   sore   sewer   soar

    1. _____

    2. _____

5 bough   bore   bare   bow

    1. _____

    2. _____

Exercise 93

Use the two given words to complete each sentence. Write the missing words on the lines.

1 forth   fourth

The hikers moved _____ for the _____ time.

2 fort   fought

The soldiers _____ to protect the _____.

3 tide   tied

We _____ the boat to the shore during high _____.

4 peer   pier

I like to _____ along the _____.

Write a sentence that uses both of the words given below.

5 bored   board

_____

6 aloud   allowed

_____

Exercise 94

For each sentence, cross out the word that is spelled incorrectly and write the correct word. Write a sentence that uses the word you crossed out correctly.

1 The prince is the air to the throne and will become king one day.

_____

2 We often go to the maul to browse through the stores.

_____

3 Be careful because the rose has a lot of thorns on its stork.

_____

4 Raj has a large brews from where he walked into the kitchen door.

_____

5 Dwayne tried to make the winning basketball shot, but he mist.

_____

6 The store agreed to wave the fee for all new customers.

_____

Exercise 95

Choose the best answer to each question.

1   Which sentence uses the underlined word correctly?
   Ⓐ   The pastry chef made a delicious <u>taut</u>.
   Ⓑ   The pastry chef made a delicious <u>tort</u>.
   Ⓒ   The pastry chef made a delicious <u>thwart</u>.
   Ⓓ   The pastry chef made a delicious <u>taught</u>.

2   Which sentence uses the underlined words correctly?
   Ⓐ   The <u>father</u> walked the bride down the <u>isle</u>.
   Ⓑ   The <u>father</u> walked the bride down the <u>aisle</u>.
   Ⓒ   The <u>farther</u> walked the bride down the <u>isle</u>.
   Ⓓ   The <u>farther</u> walked the bride down the <u>aisle</u>.

3   Which word does NOT sound the same as the other three words?
   Ⓐ   braise   Ⓒ   brays
   Ⓑ   bruise   Ⓓ   braze

4   Which word does NOT sound the same as the other three words?
   Ⓐ   pack   Ⓒ   peek
   Ⓑ   peak   Ⓓ   pique

5   Which word does NOT sound the same as the other three words?
   Ⓐ   prays   Ⓒ   prize
   Ⓑ   preys   Ⓓ   praise

Exercise 96

Write a sentence using each word. Be sure to use the correct meaning of the word in the sentence.

1 stationary _____

   stationery _____

2 presents _____

   presence _____

3 martial _____

   marshal _____

4 principal _____

   principle _____

5 chute _____

   shoot _____

6 profit _____

   prophet _____

Exercise 97

Find the word that describes what is represented by both pictures. Then write a sentence using the word. Circle the picture that uses the word in the same way as your sentence.

		Word: _____ Sentence: _____ _____
		Word: _____ Sentence: _____ _____
		Word: _____ Sentence: _____ _____
		Word: _____ Sentence: _____ _____
		Word: _____ Sentence: _____ _____

Exercise 98

Find the word that completes both sentences correctly. Write the missing words on the lines. Then write a new sentence that used the word a third way.

1 The students began to *board* the bus.

   The company held a *board* meeting.

   The surfer tried to stand up on her board.

2 Hannah put her _____ up to ask a question.

   I asked Greg for a _____ with my homework.

   _____

3 The police officer worked hard trying to solve the _____.

   I decided to take an umbrella in _____ it rained.

   _____

4 I was in a hurry, so I had to _____ breakfast.

   My two friends swung the rope, so I could learn to _____.

   _____

5 The_____ of the knife was sharper than I thought it would be.

   I kept explaining, but Cindy did not understand my _____.

   _____

Exercise 99

Find the word that matches both meanings. Then write a sentence that uses both meanings of the word.

1 a musical instrument   *fiddle*
   to muck around with something
   Lisa could fiddle with the fiddle for ages.

2 a male sheep   _____
   to hit something hard

   _____

   _____

3 the storyline of a book or movie   _____
   a field used to plant crops in

   _____

   _____

4 to go without food   _____
   to move quickly

   _____

   _____

5 a gift   _____
   the current time, now

   _____

   _____

Exercise 100

Write two sentences using each word. Use a different meaning of the word in each sentence.

 Some of the words are spelled the same, but sound different.

1 object 1. _____

2. _____

2 subject 1. _____

2. _____

3 hike 1. _____

2. _____

4 lead 1. _____

2. _____

5 down 1. _____

2. _____

6 sewer 1. _____

2. _____

Exercise 101

Many words with common uses also have newer meanings related to computers. For each word below, write a common meaning and a meaning related to computers.

1 mouse   Common: *a small animal*
           Computers: *an object used to point and click*

2 desktop   Common: _____

           Computers: _____

3 link   Common: _____

           Computers: _____

4 bookmark   Common: _____

           Computers: _____

5 browse   Common: _____

           Computers: _____

6 surf   Common: _____

           Computers: _____

Multiple Meanings Challenge

Some words that are spelled the same have many different meanings. It all depends on how the word is used. In each sentence below, the word *down* has a different meaning.

The cat is down under the table.
I put my pen down.
The machines in the factory are all down.
I tried to down the milkshake as quickly as I could.
I felt down about missing out on the game.

Each word listed below has more than two different meanings. On a separate sheet of paper, write a sentence for each meaning of the word you can think of.

Easy	Moderate	Advanced
bit	ages	second
can	close	scene
cool	lie	waste
back	pull	address
fine	space	collect
light	draw	interest
rock	blank	finish
bay	wind	object
low	let	practice

Uncommon Homophone Word Challenge

Every pair of words below sound the same, but are spelled differently. You might know the first word in each pair, but the second word is more difficult. Look up the meaning of each word you do not know. On a separate sheet of paper, write the meaning of both words in the pair and write a sentence that uses each word.

1	loot	lute
2	way	whey
3	flecks	flex
4	sink	synch
5	seed	cede
6	gate	gait
7	nice	gneiss
8	heart	hart
9	packed	pact
10	yolk	yoke
11	rough	ruff
12	you	yew
13	flew	flue
14	style	stile

Answer Key

Level 1: Exercises 1 to 10

Exercise 1
Answers: bee, pear, bear, rose, bread

Exercise 2
Any sentence that uses one of the words correctly is acceptable.
1. hear, here   2. two, too   3. wear, where   4. one, won   5. tee, tea   6. new, knew

Exercise 3
1. It hurt when **I** got sand in my **eye**.
2. I could **not** untie the **knot**.
3. Josie had always wanted to **see** the **sea**.
4. I did not **know** there was **no** milk left.
5. I **read** a book about a little **red** car.
6. I saved **four** seats **for** my friends.

Exercise 4
1. I read a funny **tale** about a bear.
2. The flag is red, white, and **blue**.
3. Jim got a letter in the **male**.
4. That is my bag over **there**.
5. I said **hi** to the bus driver.
6. I was tired, **so** I went to bed.

Exercise 5
1. C   2. A   3. B   4. C

Exercise 6
Any sentence that uses the word correctly is acceptable.

Exercise 7
Answers: star, band, roll, fan, sink, ring, ball

Exercise 8
1. bat   2. duck   3. hard   4. rock   5. bark   6. yard

Exercise 9
1. wave   2. park   3. foot or feet   4. box   5. light   6. right   7. train   8. kind

Exercise 10
Any two sentences that use a different meaning of the word are acceptable.

Level 2: Exercises 11 to 20

Exercise 11
Answers: plane, sun, tail, shoe, rain

Exercise 12
Any paragraph that uses two or more of the words is acceptable.
Answers: four, one, eight, two, pear, bean, carrot, leek

Exercise 13
1. It was not **fair** for the bus **fare** to cost so much.
2. I had to **shoo** the dog away before it took my **shoe**.
3. Emily **rode** her bike along the side of the **road**.
4. The **ad** said to **add** two dollars for postage.
5. The **hare** had brown and white **hair**.
6. There was a **rose** at the end of all the **rows** of flowers.

Exercise 14
1. My broken arm was very **sore**.
2. I **sent** a present to my aunt.
3. The tiles on the **floor** look clean.
4. I was **bored** by the long math class.
5. I **caught** the ball with my right hand.
6. Jane tried to **sell** her old bike.

Exercise 15
1. B   2. D   3. C   4. B

Exercise 16
Any sentence that uses the word correctly is acceptable.

Exercise 17
Any sentence that uses the word correctly is acceptable.
Answers: block, nail, top, row, tank

Exercise 18
1. tie   2. well   3. dear   4. cross   5. part   6. stick

Exercise 19
1. shout   2. band   3. second   4. block   5. bright   6. track   7. change   8. sink

Exercise 20
Any two sentences that use a different meaning of the word are acceptable.

Level 3: Exercises 21 to 30

Exercise 21
Any definition or picture that represents the meaning of the word is acceptable.
Answers: week, sail, cent, deer, hare

Exercise 22
Any paragraph that uses two or more of the words is acceptable.
Answers: feet, hair, ear, knee, skull, nose, waist, heel, toe, brows, fir, rose, beech, cedar

Exercise 23
1. I **saw** the bird **soar** high up into the sky.
2. I had never **seen** the movie **scene** before.
3. I **threw** the ball **through** the window.
4. The smell of the **fowl** was quite **foul**.
5. Sample answer: The **maid made** the bed.
6. Sample answer: I **ate** about **eight** grapes.

Exercise 24
Any sentence that uses the word correctly is acceptable.
1. waist   2. pale   3. pain   4. higher   5. cheep   6. raw

Exercise 25
1. A   2. B   3. B   4. C

Exercise 26
Any sentence that uses the word correctly is acceptable.

Exercise 27
Answers: line, bat, bark, fly, bill, letter, school

Exercise 28
1. even   2. face   3. top   4. blow   5. change   6. spot

Exercise 29
Any sentence that uses the word correctly is acceptable.
1. fall   2. ring   3. poor   4. watch

Exercise 30
Any two correct definitions of the word are acceptable.

Level 4: Exercises 31 to 40

Exercise 31
Any definition or picture that represents the meaning of the word is acceptable.
Answers: grate, break, beach, flower, pitcher

Exercise 32
Any sentence that uses one of the words correctly is acceptable.
1. die, dye   2. stake, steak   3. stair, stare   4. story, storey   5. mode, mowed   6. knight, night

Exercise 33
1. I forgot to **warn** Mandy that she should have **worn** a coat.
2. I could not **wait** to find out the puppy's **weight**.
3. From all the way back **here**, it is very hard to **hear**.
4. We had to **haul** the desk all the way along the **hall**.
5. Sample answer: I **heard** the **herd** of cows coming.
6. Sample answer: **We're** going to find out **where** the party is.

Exercise 34
Any sentence that uses the word correctly is acceptable.
1. read   2. flour   3. seam   4. sow   5. sense   6. wood

Exercise 35
1. D   2. A   3. C   4. A   5. A

Exercise 36
Any statement that correctly explains what the word means is acceptable.
1. what   2. band   3. earn   4. few   5. spa   6. lone

Exercise 37
Any sentence that uses the word correctly is acceptable.
Answers: cross, chop, web, match, shake

Exercise 38
1. iron   2. cave   3. mind   4. handle   5. broke   6. shot

Exercise 39
1. bill   2. plate   3. tap   4. break   5. chest   6. note   7. model   8. inch

Exercise 40
Any two sentences that use a different meaning of the word are acceptable.

Level 5: Exercises 41 to 50

Exercise 41
Answers: claws, knight, jeans, miner, links

Exercise 42
Any paragraph that uses three or more of the words is acceptable.
Answers: bear, flea, hare, bee, ewe, toad, fowl, horse, whale, mite, boar, deer, gnu, tern

Exercise 43
1. The boat sailed **straight** along the **strait**.
2. The **fax** contains all the **facts** you'll need to know.
3. I felt **tense** about getting the **tents** up in time.
4. The king's **throne** was **thrown** away.
5. Sample answer: The baby will **bawl** if you take his **ball**.
6. Sample answer: **They're** going to miss **their** bus.

Exercise 44
Any sentence that uses the word correctly is acceptable.
1. rays   2. nor   3. meddle   4. seem   5. sew   6. peak

Exercise 45
1. B   2. D   3. B   4. D   5. A

Exercise 46
Any statement that correctly explains what the word means is acceptable.
1. neigh   2. more   3. turn   4. real   5. we   6. alter

Exercise 47
Answers: fork, rock, watch, box, train, ruler, pin

Exercise 48
1. ages   2. lead   3. lift   4. pound   5. rich   6. plain

Exercise 49
Any sentence that uses the word correctly is acceptable.
1. save   2. clear   3. faint   4. post

Exercise 50
Any two correct definitions of the word are acceptable.

Level 6: Exercises 51 to 60

Exercise 51
Answers: isle, mussel, quartz, throne, yolk

Exercise 52
Any sentence that uses one of the words correctly is acceptable.
1. bread, bred   2. hail, hale   3. sent, scent   4. piece, peace   5. sight, site   6. hour, our

Exercise 53
1. The golfer had to yell **fore** at least **four** times.
2. The **main** thing I noticed about the lion was its **mane**.
3. Chloe **might** have been bitten by a **mite**.
4. After a short **pause** the cat continued to lick its **paws**.
5. Sample answer: Of **course** the sand was **coarse**.
6. Sample answer: The **plane** landed on the **plain**.

Exercise 54
Any sentence that uses the first word correctly is acceptable.
1. coarse → course   2. sauce → source   3. belle → bell
4. desert → dessert   5. whole → hole   6. tide → tied

Exercise 55
1. A   2. C   3. C   4. C   5. B

Exercise 56
Any sentence that uses the correct meaning of the word is acceptable.

Exercise 57
1. just   2. flock   3. long   4. scoop   5. spell   6. type

Exercise 58
1. B   2. D   3. C   4. C   5. A   6. B

Exercise 59
Any two correct definitions of the word are acceptable.

Exercise 60
Any two sentences that correctly use the word as a noun and a verb are acceptable.

Level 7: Exercises 61 to 70

Exercise 61
Any sentence that uses the correct meaning of the word is acceptable.
Answers: knot, flea, witch, weigh, hail, plum

Exercise 62
Any paragraph that uses three or more of the words is acceptable.
Answers: meat, berry, steak, maize, pie, thyme, jam, bread, beet, cereal, dough, roll, sundae, currant

Exercise 63
1. I **guessed** that the secret **guest** was my aunt.
2. The gold **miner** only had a **minor** injury.
3. I did not know **whether** the **weather** would be nice.
4. The bridge crossing the **creek** began to **creak**.
5. Sample answer: I **rode** my bike down the **road**.
6. Sample answer: The **right** thing to do is to **write** a note.

Exercise 64
Any sentence that uses the first word correctly is acceptable.
1. idle → idol
2. whirr → were
3. ewe → you
4. boarder → border
5. cellar → seller
6. owed → ode

Exercise 65
1. C   2. B   3. C   4. D   5. B

Exercise 66
Any sentence that uses the correct meaning of the word is acceptable.

Exercise 67
Any sentence that uses the word correctly is acceptable.
Answers: notes, bow, dummy, seal, cut

Exercise 68
1. cells   2. fit   3. jam   4. shock   5. sign   6. force

Exercise 69
1. cast   2. crow   3. marble   4. gum   5. check   6. bank   7. beams   8. firm

Exercise 70
Any two sentences that use a different meaning of the word are acceptable.

Level 8: Exercises 71 to 80

Exercise 71
Any sentence that uses the correct meaning of the word is acceptable.
Answers: add, whale, wave, stare, bite, pole

Exercise 72
Any statement that correctly explains what the word means is acceptable.
1. deer, dear   2. wrap, rap   3. raise, rays   4. flea, flee   5. floor, flaw

Exercise 73
1. I felt sick and **weak** for most of last **week**.
2. The potato and **leek** soup began to **leak** everywhere.
3. The paths through the field of **maize** were like a **maze**.
4. Craig was upset to **find** he had been **fined** for speeding.
5. Sample answer: It is **your** job to make sure **you're** ready.
6. Sample answer: I **would** like help to cut the **wood**.

Exercise 74
Any sentence that uses the word correctly is acceptable.
1. world 2. dual 3. barren 4. tacks 5. boulder 6. choose

Exercise 75
1. B   2. D   3. C   4. C   5. A

Exercise 76
Any sentence that uses the correct meaning of the word is acceptable.

Exercise 77
Any third sentence that uses an additional meaning of the word is acceptable.
1. spring 2. scale 3. rock 4. line 5. fine

Exercise 78
1. B   2. C   3. B   4. C   5. A   6. D

Exercise 79
Any two sentences that use a different meaning of the word are acceptable.

Exercise 80
Any two sentences that correctly use the word as a noun and a verb are acceptable.

Level 9: Exercises 81 to 90

Exercise 81
Any sentence that uses the correct meaning of the word is acceptable.
Answers: moose, ferry, urn, pail, herd, reel

Exercise 82
Any paragraph that uses three or more of the words is acceptable.
Answers: aunt, nun, beau, belle, witch, son, colonel, prophet, guest, heir, boy, maid, prince, knight, juggler, idol

Exercise 83
1. Maxwell joined the **queue** right on **cue**.
2. We are **due** for a cold morning with **dew**.
3. The motorcycle jumping 300 **feet** was an amazing **feat**.
4. The squirrel often **buries** nuts and **berries**.
5. Sample answer: I am not **sure** if I want to go to the **shore**.
6. Sample answer: **We'll** check the front **wheel** later.

Exercise 84
Any sentence that uses the first word correctly is acceptable.
1. key → quay
2. beau → bow
3. buoys → boys
4. dense → dents
5. phrase → frays
6. lapse → laps

Exercise 85
1. B   2. D   3. D   4. A   5. B

Exercise 86
Any statement that correctly explains what the word means is acceptable.
1. row 2. jewel 3. lava 4. tuba 5. tears 6. soared 7. fur

Exercise 87
Any sentence that uses the word correctly is acceptable.
Answers: drive, point, tape, basket, cycle

Exercise 88
1. A   2. C   3. B   4. D   5. A   6. C

Exercise 89
Any sentence that uses the word correctly is acceptable.
1. minute   2. patient   3. pet   4. dove

Exercise 90
Any set of statements that give correct meanings of the word are acceptable.

Level 10: Exercises 91 to 101

Exercise 91
Any sentence that uses the correct meaning of the word is acceptable.
Answers: peel, sweet, root, pedal, court, maze

Exercise 92
Any statement that correctly explains what the word means is acceptable.
1. lone, loan   2. steal, steel   3. beet, beat   4. sore, soar   5. bough, bow

Exercise 93
1. The hikers moved **forth** for the **fourth** time.   2. The soldiers **fought** to protect the **fort**.
3. We **tied** the boat to the shore during high **tide**.   4. I like to **peer** along the **pier**.
5. Sample answer: Looking at the **board** made me feel **bored**.
6. Sample answer: We are not **allowed** to say the answers **aloud**.

Exercise 94
Any sentence that uses the first word correctly is acceptable.
1. air → heir   2. maul → mall   3. stork → stalk
4. brews → bruise   5. mist → missed   6. wave → waive

Exercise 95
1. B   2. B   3. B   4. A   5. C

Exercise 96
Any sentence that uses the correct meaning of the word is acceptable.

Exercise 97
Any sentence that uses the word correctly is acceptable.
Answers: file, scales, branch, state, charge

Exercise 98
Any third sentence that uses an additional meaning of the word is acceptable.
1. board   2. hand   3. case   4. skip   5. point

Exercise 99
Any sentence that uses both meanings of the word is acceptable.
1. fiddle   2. ram   3. plot   4. fast   5. present

Exercise 100
Any two sentences that use a different meaning of the word are acceptable.

Exercise 101
Any set of statements that give correct common and computer-related meanings of the word are acceptable.

Common Core Standards Alignment

The Common Core Standards are a set of standards adopted by most American states. The standards describe what students are expected to be able to do, and list the skills that students learn. Student learning is based on these standards throughout the year, and students in most states are tested based on these standards at the end of the school year.

The Common Core Standards for English Language Arts are divided into reading, writing, speaking and listening, and language. The list below describes the specific skills in the standards that are addressed in this workbook.

Strand	Skill Addressed
Language	<ul><li>Correctly use frequently confused words.</li><li>Understand and use verbs and nouns.</li><li>Use an apostrophe to form contractions.</li><li>Use spelling patterns and generalizations in writing words.</li><li>Spell grade-appropriate words correctly, consulting references as needed.</li><li>Determine or clarify the meaning of unknown and multiple-meaning words and phrases.</li><li>Use sentence-level context as a clue to the meaning of a word or phrase.</li><li>Use context (e.g., definitions, examples, or restatements in text) as a clue to the meaning of a word or phrase.</li><li>Use glossaries and dictionaries to determine or clarify the meaning of words.</li><li>Distinguish the literal and nonliteral meanings of words and phrases in context.</li><li>Identify real-life connections between words and their use.</li><li>Use the relationship between particular words (e.g., synonyms, antonyms, homographs) to better understand each of the words.</li><li>Acquire and use words and phrases acquired through conversations, reading and being read to, and responding to texts.</li></ul>
Reading	<ul><li>Know and apply grade-level phonics and word analysis skills in decoding words.</li><li>Know spelling-sound correspondences for common vowel teams.</li><li>Recognize and read grade-appropriate irregularly spelled words.</li><li>Decode regularly spelled words.</li><li>Identify words with inconsistent but common spelling-sound correspondences.</li><li>Use combined knowledge of all letter-sound correspondences, syllabication patterns, and morphology to read accurately in context and out of context.</li><li>Determine the meaning of words and phrases as they are used in a text.</li><li>Determine word meaning, distinguishing literal from non-literal language.</li><li>Use context to confirm or self-correct word recognition and understanding, rereading as necessary.</li></ul>
Writing	<ul><li>Develop and strengthen writing as needed by planning, revising, and editing.</li><li>Write routinely over extended time frames and shorter time frames for a range of discipline-specific tasks, purposes, and audiences.</li></ul>

Made in the USA
Lexington, KY
19 January 2018